"I am not a racist. I am against every form of racism and segregation, every form of discrimination. I believe in human beings, and that all human beings should be respected as such, regardless of their color."

—MALCOLM X, JANUARY 18, 1965

MALCOLM X

BY THERESA CRUSHSHON

The Child's World

MALCOLM X WAS ASSASSINATED IN 1965, BUT HE LEFT BEHIND IDEAS THAT CONTINUE TO INSPIRE PEOPLE TODAY.

Malcolm Little

Malcolm X was **assassinated** in February of 1965, when he was only 39 years old. Even by that age, his life and his view of the world had changed many times. He had already accomplished a great deal. As a religious and political leader, he was a powerful voice in American history who fought **discrimination.** He inspired many African Americans to join the struggle for **civil rights,** but he believed that blacks should strive for more than just equality. He believed they should also build pride in and respect for their own culture. He believed that self-respect and independence were the two most important qualities a person could possess.

For many years, Malcolm X was a **militant** who spoke out fiercely and angrily against **racism.** He told African Americans to demand better treatment, even if they had to use violence to get it. At first, Malcolm X did not believe that blacks could end racism by working peacefully with white people. He believed that the races must remain separate. But toward the end of his life, his views began to change. He realized that violence would never be the best way to fight **injustice.** He had begun to explain his new point of view just before his death.

Malcolm was born on May 19, 1925, in Omaha, Nebraska. His parents were Earl and Louise Little. (Malcolm Little changed his name to Malcolm X as an adult.) Earl Little was a Baptist minister who came from Georgia. In his first marriage, Earl had three children. Earl married Louise, Malcolm's mother, in 1919. Malcolm was the fourth child. The Littles had four more children, so Malcolm grew up in a large family. He would always be especially close to his half-sister, Ella. Although Malcolm came from a happy family, his childhood was not easy.

Malcolm grew up in troubled times. Black people in the United States did not have the same rights as white Americans. Schools and public places were often **segregated,** with the races kept apart. Black men and women were barred from many jobs. In some places, African Americans were not allowed to vote. Worst of all, blacks were often victims of hatred and even violence. Slavery had been outlawed for more than 60 years, but African Americans were not truly free. Most opportunities for a good life still were not available to them.

Many African Americans wanted to change this situation. One man who hoped to make a difference was Marcus Garvey. Born in Jamaica, Garvey moved to New York City, where he founded the Universal Negro Improvement Association (UNIA). UNIA supported black-owned businesses and any ventures that would help black people succeed in life. But Garvey also believed that black people would never have equal rights in the United States. He wanted to help African Americans return to what he called their motherland—the continent of Africa. Other black leaders disagreed. They believed that African Americans should focus on making their lives better in the United States. But thousands of African Americans, including Malcolm's father, agreed with Garvey. Garvey's ideas would influence Malcolm one day as well.

By the time Malcolm was born, Garvey was no longer the head of UNIA, but Earl Little still believed in Garvey's teachings. Earl believed that African Americans must demand an end to the injustice they suffered. In his free time, Earl talked to other African Americans about his beliefs. He encouraged them to fight for equality. When Malcolm was still a baby, his family received threats because of Earl's beliefs. Earl and Louise decided to move to Michigan, hoping to find a better life.

In Lansing, Michigan, Earl bought a house for his family. He continued to work as a preacher while Louise cared for the children. They both hoped they had found a good place in which to raise their family. Earl's commitment to his beliefs had not changed. He continued to speak out against racism.

Earl Little told the African Americans of Lansing that they should refuse to live as second-class citizens. It didn't take long for white townspeople to notice the outspoken newcomer. To them, Little was a troublemaker who would encourage other blacks to demand change.

Although Malcolm's childhood was difficult, he did have some happy times. He enjoyed playing with his brothers and sisters, and he loved and admired his parents. As a little boy, Malcolm enjoyed gardening. His mother gave him a special place in the yard where he could plant seeds. Malcolm liked peas, so he planted rows and rows of them. He loved to see his homegrown peas on the dinner table.

Library of Congress

MARCUS GARVEY (ABOVE) FOUNDED THE UNIVERSAL NEGRO IMPROVEMENT ASSOCIATION, A WORLDWIDE ORGANIZATION DEDICATED TO RACIAL PRIDE AND INDEPENDENCE FOR BLACK PEOPLE. EARL LITTLE RESPECTED GARVEY'S IDEAS. MANY YEARS LATER, THEY WOULD INSPIRE HIS SON MALCOLM AS WELL.

The Schomburg Center

TAKING A STAND AGAINST RACISM WAS DANGEROUS, BUT EARL LITTLE (RIGHT) BELIEVED AFRICAN AMERICANS MUST FIGHT INJUSTICE IN ANY WAY THEY COULD. HE AND MALCOLM'S MOTHER, LOUISE (LEFT), STRUGGLED TO MAKE A GOOD LIFE FOR THEIR CHILDREN, BUT THE FAMILY WAS OFTEN THREATENED WITH VIOLENCE BECAUSE OF EARL'S BELIEFS.

Malcolm also had terrible moments in his early years. In 1929, when he was only four, the Littles' home was burned to the ground. Some of Lansing's white townspeople wanted to scare Earl Little or perhaps even to kill him. As the family slept, a group of men set fire to the house. The house filled with smoke, and the Littles, fearing for their lives, ran outside. White police officers and firefighters stood and watched as the Littles' home went up in flames. No one offered a bucket of water, and no one was arrested for the crime. The memory of this terrible event stayed with Malcolm forever.

After the fire the Littles no longer had a home, so they lived with friends for a short time. Soon they moved to the outskirts of East Lansing. Malcolm enjoyed walking on the hills surrounding the city. As he grew bigger, he liked reading, playing basketball, fishing, and trapping rabbits.

MALCOLM IS SHOWN HERE AS A YOUNG BOY. HIS CHILDHOOD WAS DIFFICULT, AND HE FACED RACISM AND VIOLENCE WHILE HE WAS STILL VERY YOUNG. THESE EXPERIENCES REMAINED WITH HIM FOREVER.

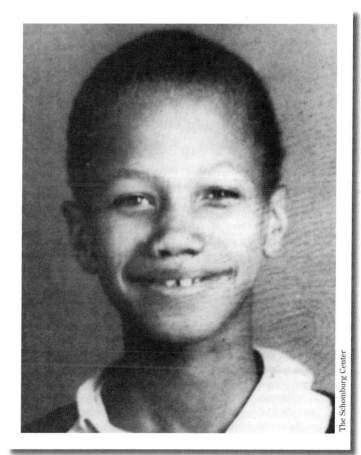

The Schomburg Center

Malcolm had both good and bad memories of school. He attended Lansing's Pleasant Grove Elementary School. Only a few black children went there. His classmates liked him and Malcolm earned good grades, but he still experienced racism at school. Some of the students and even a few teachers called him names like "nigger" or "darkie." One day, Malcolm told a teacher that he wanted to become a lawyer. His teacher laughed. He said that law was not a career for a black person and that Malcolm should plan to become a carpenter instead.

Soon after Malcolm started school, another tragedy struck his family. On September 28, 1931, Earl Little was found dead. He had been run over by a streetcar. Some people in Lansing's African American community believed that Little had been murdered.

They said that white men had severely beaten him, then dragged his body onto the streetcar tracks so that the death would look like an accident. No one ever investigated these charges to determine whether they were true.

The death of Earl Little took a terrible toll on his family. Louise had always depended on him. Now she was left with eight children to feed. It was difficult for her to find work. She was a proud woman who hated the idea of needing help, but with no job, she had to accept **welfare** from the state.

Pleasant Grove Elementary School

MALCOLM IS SHOWN HERE (THIRD FROM RIGHT IN THE BACK ROW)
WITH HIS FOURTH-GRADE CLASS AT PLEASANT GROVE ELEMENTARY
SCHOOL IN LANSING, MICHIGAN.

AFTER HIS FATHER'S DEATH, MALCOLM (SHOWN ABOVE AT AGE 14) BEGAN TO GET INTO TROUBLE. HE SOON LEFT MICHIGAN, TRAVELING TO BOSTON AND THEN HARLEM IN SEARCH OF EXCITEMENT.

A Rude Awakening

Times became more and more difficult for Malcolm's family. They often had no money for groceries, so they ate boiled dandelion greens or whatever else they could find. Sometimes Malcolm was so hungry, he felt dizzy. Louise had trouble controlling her children, and they began to get into trouble. Louise became so unhappy that her health suffered. In 1939, she had a **breakdown** and was sent to a hospital. Later that year, Malcolm and the rest of her young children were sent to live in foster homes. Louise Little spent the next 26 years in the hospital.

Malcolm remained close to his brothers and sisters, even though they lived apart. During one summer vacation, he went to visit his half-sister Ella in Boston. He liked life in the big city, with its bright lights and fast cars. He returned to Michigan for only a short time before dropping out of school. Then he moved to Boston to live with Ella and her husband. Malcolm worked hard to be "cool" like the young men who had grown up in the city. He began using slang words. He also changed his appearance, straightening his curly hair and wearing wild fashions.

In Boston, Malcolm found a job shining shoes at the Roseland State Ballroom, where big bands played. He met famous musicians such as Duke Ellington and Count Basie. In 1942, he moved to Harlem, an African American neighborhood in New York City. In Harlem, Malcolm was known as "Red" because his hair was a reddish color. He became a small-time criminal. He also started to gamble and use drugs. When he made enemies in Harlem, Malcolm returned to Boston. He joined a burglary gang that broke into houses. Malcolm feared nothing, but eventually his luck ran out. In 1946, he was arrested and sentenced to 10 years in prison.

Life was hard in Boston's Charlestown State Prison. Malcolm's bare cell was tiny and had no running water. He had plenty of time to think about what he had done to his life.

In prison, Malcolm felt great anger and cursed at the prison workers. He yelled a lot, and his cellmates started calling him "Satan." Although it was a difficult time in his life, Malcolm later realized that it was also the beginning of a **transformation.** "I don't think anyone ever got as much out of going to prison as I did," he later wrote.

While in jail, Malcolm met a man named Bimbi. Bimbi spent many hours reading and thinking, and the other prisoners respected him. He was one of the first educated black men Malcolm had ever met. Bimbi's knowledge impressed him. Following Bimbi's example, Malcolm began to educate himself. He checked out books from the prison library and spent hours studying. Reading opened up a new world to Malcolm. It increased his vocabulary, and his confidence grew.

IN BOSTON, MALCOLM (SHOWN ABOVE AT AGE 15) TRIED TO DRESS AND ACT LIKE THE "COOL" KIDS HE MET IN THE BIG CITY. HE WORE TRENDY CLOTHES, LIKE THE "ZOOT SUIT" SHOWN IN THIS PHOTO. ZOOT SUITS, WITH THEIR LONG JACKETS AND WIDE LEGS, WERE POPULAR AMONG HIS CROWD.

Boston Public Library

AFTER HE WAS CONVICTED OF BURGLARY, MALCOLM WAS SENT TO CHARLESTOWN STATE PRISON, SHOWN ABOVE. LIFE IN PRISON WAS DIFFICULT FOR HIM AT FIRST. BUT BY 1948, HE WAS TRANSFERRED TO NORFOLK PRISON COLONY, WHICH WAS A BETTER PLACE TO BE. HE HAD ALSO BEGUN STUDYING AND LEARNING ABOUT THE NATION OF ISLAM, AND HIS LIFE TOOK A DRAMATIC TURN FOR THE BETTER.

In 1948, Malcolm was transferred to Norfolk Prison Colony, a newer prison. At Norfolk, the inmates shared small houses. They had running water, their own rooms, and an excellent library. Malcolm spent four years at the prison. He continued to read, and his progress was impressive.

By this time, Malcolm had started to learn about the Nation of **Islam.** Islam is an ancient religion that started in the Middle East. Its followers are called Muslims. They follow strict rules for life set out in the holy book called the Koran. Muslims believe that God gave the wisdom in the Koran to Muhammad, a **prophet.** Muhammad began to preach in A.D. 613. Since that time, Islam has spread all over the world. During the 1940s, many African Americans began to join the organization known as the Nation of Islam. Its members are known as Black Muslims. The Nation of Islam built temples and **mosques,** Islamic places of worship, all over the United States.

At the time, the Nation of Islam's leader was Elijah Muhammad, named after the great Muslim prophet. Elijah Muhammad talked not only about Islamic teachings but also about the plight of African Americans. He based many of his teachings on the work of Marcus Garvey. For one thing, Elijah Muhammad believed that whites and blacks should remain apart. He wanted blacks in the United States to break free from what he called a dangerous society controlled by white people. He said that black people should build their own society, apart from other races. Elijah Muhammad argued that whites were evil people who wanted African Americans to remain ignorant and **oppressed.**

Elijah Muhammad and the Nation of Islam scared many white Americans. Many African Americans, however, responded to their message. Like Malcolm, some were prisoners who were helped by the teachings of the Nation of Islam. Law-abiding members of the African American community joined the Nation as well.

Malcolm first learned about Elijah Muhammad and his teachings when his brother visited him in prison. He learned more through books and by talking to Black Muslims he met in prison.

Malcolm began to write letters to Elijah Muhammad and faithfully follow Islam's strict rules. He promised to give up drugs and alcohol. He also took a vow of poverty, saying that after he left prison and got a job, he would give most of his earnings to his mosque.

In 1952, Malcolm was released from prison. He went to Chicago to visit Elijah Muhammad. He then moved to Detroit, where he became a member of a Nation of Islam temple. By that time, Malcolm had dropped his last name, Little, and replaced it with an X. He said that "Little" was not truly his family name. Instead, it was a slave name, given to his ancestors by white slave owners. Malcolm used the X to refer to his unknown African name, the one taken from his relatives when they were brought to America. Other Black Muslims use an X in the same way.

WHEN MALCOLM LEARNED ABOUT THE NATION OF ISLAM, ELIJAH MUHAMMAD (RIGHT) WAS THE ORGANIZATION'S LEADER. MALCOLM SOON BECAME A DEVOTED FOLLOWER OF ELIJAH MUHAMMAD. WHEN MALCOLM WAS RELEASED FROM PRISON, MUHAMMAD HELPED HIM GAIN INFLUENCE WITHIN THE NATION OF ISLAM.

Corbis

MALCOLM QUICKLY ROSE TO A POSITION OF LEADER-
SHIP WITHIN THE NATION OF ISLAM. HE RECRUITED
NEW MEMBERS TO THE ORGANIZATION AND SERVED AS
THE MINISTER OF MOSQUES IN HARLEM, DETROIT,
AND PHILADELPHIA.

A Civil Rights Leader

In Detroit, Malcolm X soon became a leader of the Nation of Islam. He became a religious leader at his mosque and started to **recruit** new members to the Nation of Islam. He became a spokesperson for the organization, which was growing quickly. He also met a woman named Betty Sanders (who later changed her name to Betty Shabazz). Malcolm and Betty married in January of 1958 and moved to Queens, New York.

In the mid-1950s, the **Civil Rights Movement** spread across the United States. In 1954, the **Supreme Court** ruled that schools could no longer be segregated. For years, people in southern states had argued that their segregated schools were "separate but equal." They claimed that even if black people could not attend white schools, they had their own schools that offered the same ("equal") classes. African Americans disagreed. For one thing, schools for blacks were usually inferior. There also were fewer of them, so black children often had to travel long distances to attend class. The Supreme Court agreed that "separate but equal" was not good enough, and segregation was outlawed in public schools. This decision inspired African Americans to fight for other rights, too.

The following year, the Civil Rights Movement found a hero, a woman named Rosa Parks. Parks lived in Montgomery, Alabama. One day in 1955, she was on her way home from work when the bus driver told her to give up her seat to a white passenger. Laws at that time said that black people must give up their bus seats to whites. When Parks refused, she was arrested.

A Baptist preacher and political leader came to her assistance. His name was the Reverend Martin Luther King Jr. He later became one of the greatest leaders of the Civil Rights Movement.

King wanted black people to have equal rights but did not believe they should use violence to get them. He believed deeply in **nonviolence,** achieving a goal without hurting others.

To support Parks, King and other African Americans organized a **boycott** of the Montgomery bus system. For more than a year, they refused to ride Montgomery buses. Finally, on December 20, 1956, the Supreme Court ordered Montgomery to **integrate** its public bus lines. The bus company's segregation rules were now illegal. The black citizens of Montgomery had won!

This success encouraged more African Americans to join the Civil Rights Movement. Malcolm X and many other members of the Nation of Islam supported the movement. But Malcolm X did not believe, as Reverend King and other civil rights leaders did, that African Americans should try to become part of white society. He still wanted African Americans to remain separate and build their own society.

Malcolm X also believed that King's idea of nonviolence was a mistake. He said blacks should fight back in self-defense whenever necessary. "I firmly believe," he said, "that Negroes have the right [to fight] against … racists by any means necessary." People began to compare King and Malcolm X. King was the peaceful, reasonable side of the Civil Rights Movement. Malcolm X was its angry, militant side. While many Americans—black and white—respected Reverend King, they feared Malcolm X and his ideas.

Malcolm X continued to build the membership of the Nation of Islam. By 1963, more than 30,000 African Americans had joined. Thousands more supported its efforts. Malcolm X was a public figure. He gave fiery speeches. Newspapers published articles about him, and television news reporters talked about him. When white Americans heard what Malcolm X had to say, many considered him a dangerous man. Some people said he was a racist. After all, he spoke angrily about white people.

Corbis

MANY PEOPLE BELIEVE THE MONTGOMERY BUS BOYCOTT WAS THE BEGINNING OF THE CIVIL RIGHTS MOVEMENT. ROSA PARKS IS SHOWN HERE ON A MONTGOMERY BUS AFTER THE SUPREME COURT ORDERED THE CITY TO INTEGRATE ITS BUSES.

Corbis

MARTIN LUTHER KING (ABOVE) WAS THE MOST FAMOUS LEADER OF THE CIVIL RIGHTS MOVEMENT. HIS VIEWS DIFFERED GREATLY FROM THOSE OF MALCOLM X. KING'S GOAL WAS THE PEACEFUL INTEGRATION OF BLACKS INTO AMERICAN SOCIETY. BUT MALCOLM X SAID, "IT IS NOT INTEGRATION THAT NEGROES IN AMERICA WANT, IT IS HUMAN DIGNITY."

Malcolm X wanted blacks and whites to remain separate. Many people wondered about this message. Was the separation he spoke of any different from the segregation that civil rights leaders such as Martin Luther King were fighting against?

As Malcolm X grew more famous, the FBI began to investigate him. He was not concerned, however. He continued speaking openly about racism and the Nation of Islam. He still claimed that violence was acceptable if it was the only way to achieve freedom, equality, and independence for African Americans. About King's ideal of nonviolence, Malcolm X said, "It is criminal to teach a man not to defend himself when he is the constant victim of brutal attacks."

Over time, Malcolm X and Elijah Muhammad began to disagree on many issues. Muhammad believed Malcolm X was too **radical.**

Library of Congress

MALCOLM X BECAME INCREASINGLY FAMOUS AS A PUBLIC SPEAKER, AND HIS FAME BROUGHT NATIONAL ATTENTION TO THE NATION OF ISLAM. BUT HIS IDEAS FRIGHTENED MANY PEOPLE, AND THE FBI BEGAN TO INVESTIGATE HIM.

Corbis

MALCOLM X BEGAN TO DISAGREE WITH THE TEACHINGS OF ELIJAH MUHAMMAD, BUT MANY AFRICAN AMERICANS CONTINUED TO SUPPORT THE BLACK MUSLIMS. ONE FAMOUS FOLLOWER OF ELIJAH MUHAMMAD WAS THE WORLD HEAVYWEIGHT BOXING CHAMPION, MUHAMMAD ALI, SHOWN HERE SPEAKING AT A MEETING OF THE BLACK MUSLIMS. SEATED AT RIGHT IS ELIJAH MUHAMMAD.

Elijah Muhammad did not share the idea that violence might be necessary and even acceptable. In turn, Malcolm X began to reject some of the beliefs of the Nation of Islam. For one thing, Muhammad claimed that white people were created not by God, but by a mad scientist. Malcolm X refused to believe this.

The division between the two men grew more serious after the assassination of President John Kennedy in November of 1963. Elijah Muhammad had told members of the Nation of Islam not to comment on Kennedy's death. But Malcolm X did not obey. When a reporter asked Malcolm his feelings about the assassination, he said, "The hate in white men had not stopped with the killing of defenseless black people, but the hate, allowed to spread unchecked, finally had struck down this country's chief of state."

When Elijah Muhammad heard what Malcolm X had said, he ordered him not to speak in public. Malcolm began to think about whether he truly believed the teachings of the Nation of Islam. He decided it was time to move on. Malcolm X was ready to become the leader of his own organization.

Corbis

THE ASSASSINATION OF U.S. PRESIDENT JOHN F. KENNEDY (LEFT) CAUSED FURTHER DISAGREEMENT BETWEEN ELIJAH MUHAMMAD AND MALCOLM X.

ON MARCH 8, 1964, MALCOLM X ANNOUNCED THAT HE WAS LEAVING THE NATION OF ISLAM TO FORM THE MUSLIM MOSQUE. HIS GOAL WAS TO HELP AFRICAN AMERICANS TAKE CONTROL OF THEIR COMMUNITIES AND GAIN INDEPENDENCE.

Another Transformation

In March of 1964, Malcolm X broke away from the Nation of Islam. At a public meeting in Harlem, New York, he said he was starting a new Islamic organization. He called it Muslim Mosque. He told reporters that it would be a religious group, but he talked even more about his "action program." He hoped to promote a program that would help African Americans gain control of their own communities. He said blacks should play an active role in the government. He also thought they should strive for **economic** independence by opening and supporting their own businesses. Black people should see black doctors. Schools in black neighborhoods should hire black teachers. By taking such actions, Malcolm argued, black people would have the means to become independent and successful. They could take control of their own lives.

After founding the Muslim Mosque, Malcolm X went on a **pilgrimage.** According to Islamic beliefs, each Muslim is supposed to make at least one trip to the city of Mecca in Saudi Arabia. Mecca is the city where the prophet Muhammad was born. To Muslims, it is the holiest of places. Malcolm X also planned to visit other places with large Muslim populations, including several Middle Eastern and African countries.

Malcolm X's journey would be the start of another great transformation in his life. He began his pilgrimage in Cairo, Egypt. Many other Muslims from all over the world were there, preparing to make the same trip to Mecca. They exchanged their everyday clothes for the plain clothing of Muslim pilgrims. Then they flew to Saudi Arabia. Once in Mecca, Malcolm X went to the Great Mosque, where Muslims gather to worship.

During his journey, Malcolm X learned a great deal about the traditional religion of Islam. He learned that it was very different from the religion the Nation of Islam practiced. He also realized that people of all races, not just black people, were Muslim. He later wrote that there were people of every color in Mecca: "white, black, brown, red, and yellow people, blue eyes and blonde hair, and my kinky red hair—all together, brothers! All honoring the same God Allah, all in turn giving equal honor to the other." In Mecca, no one was judged by the color of his or her skin.

Corbis

MECCA IS THE MOST SACRED OF MUSLIM HOLY CITIES. HERE, THOUSANDS OF PILGRIMS ARE SHOWN GATHERING AT EL HARAM, THE GREAT MOSQUE IN MECCA, DURING AN ANNUAL GATHERING OF MUSLIM FAITHFUL. ALL MUSLIMS ARE SUPPOSED TO VISIT MECCA AT LEAST ONCE IN THEIR LIVES. MALCOLM X VISITED THE HOLY CITY IN 1964.

When the time came for Malcolm X to go home, other pilgrims asked him what had impressed him most during his journey. He said it was the brotherhood he had witnessed. He wrote a letter to friends and family that was published in the newspapers. In it he described the people he had seen worshiping together. He realized that blacks and whites could live and work together. He signed the letter in a new way. The man who had called himself Malcolm X now used a Muslim name, El-Hajj Malik El-Shabazz. Most Americans continued to call him Malcolm X, and he did not object.

After his pilgrimage, Malcolm X went to Africa. There he learned about Pan-Africanism, the idea that black people around the world would one day unite as a single, strong community. He became interested in this idea and planned to talk about it in the United States. Finally, he returned home to New York.

Malcolm X had changed during his journey. He was more open-minded. He no longer believed that people of different races should remain separate. He continued to believe that racism was a serious problem—so serious that it could destroy the United States. But he now realized that people of different races could live together if they shared common ideals and beliefs. He saw new and positive ways to fight oppression.

For the first time, Malcolm X began to work with other black leaders, such as members of the National Association for the Advancement of Colored People (NAACP). He also met with Martin Luther King. He even began to say that white people could take part in the black freedom movement. His new attitude was made clear when he told a news reporter, "The 22 million Afro-Americans don't seek either separation or integration. They seek recognition and respect as human beings." Malcolm X now encouraged blacks to work with each other —and even with people of other races— to end discrimination.

Malcolm X also started the Organization of Afro-American Unity (OAAU). The OAAU was not a religious group. Its goal was to help blacks defend themselves against oppression and unite with people in Africa. It was the first step in his plan to encourage Pan-Africanism. Malcolm also hoped the OAAU would help African Americans gain economic and political control of their communities. It encouraged black Americans to vote and to take part in politics.

Shortly after Malcolm X had returned from his pilgrimage, a famous journalist named Alex Haley approached him. Haley asked whether Malcolm would like to tell his story in a book. Malcolm agreed, and the two men met often to talk. Haley recorded what Malcolm X told him about both his personal life and his ideas. The book would be published in 1965 as *The Autobiography of Malcolm X.*

Not everyone approved of Malcolm X's new ideas. Some people believed that he had betrayed the Nation of Islam. He began to receive death threats.

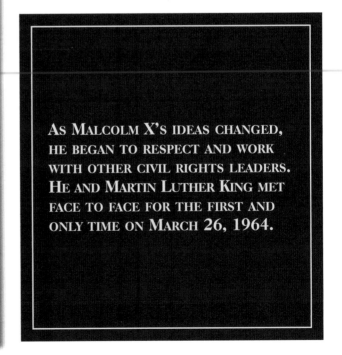

Corbis

AS MALCOLM X'S IDEAS CHANGED, HE BEGAN TO RESPECT AND WORK WITH OTHER CIVIL RIGHTS LEADERS. HE AND MARTIN LUTHER KING MET FACE TO FACE FOR THE FIRST AND ONLY TIME ON MARCH 26, 1964.

Despite the threats, Malcolm X continued to reach out to people without fear. But by late 1964, he began to fear that a serious attempt might be made on his life. He even asked for police protection, but it was not granted. On February 14, 1965, homemade bombs were thrown into Malcolm X's home in the middle of the night. He, his pregnant wife, and their children were asleep inside. They were lucky to escape with their lives. At a public meeting two days later, Malcolm X accused Nation of Islam members of throwing the bombs. The worst was yet to come.

Library of Congress

On February 14, 1965, bombs were thrown into Malcolm X's home in Elmhurst, New York. The bombs damaged the house and furniture and frightened the family. Although no one was hurt, Malcolm X feared that more violence was to come.

A week later, on Sunday, February 21, 1965, Malcolm X and his family went to a New York City meeting hall where he was scheduled to give a speech to the OAAU. He walked into the room, where a crowd had gathered. He had just begun to speak when three men stood up and rushed toward the stage. They pulled out guns and fired several shots at Malcolm X. Everyone in the room ran for cover, but Malcolm had no time to hide. Sixteen bullets struck his body. He fell over backward and hit the floor. His wife ran to him, but she knew at once that he was dead.

Police officers ran into the building. Members of the crowd had captured one suspect, and the police took him into custody. Someone had run to a nearby hospital and returned with a stretcher. Malcolm X was carried to the emergency room, but it was too late. Malcolm X was dead. Three Black Muslims would later be tried and convicted for his murder.

News of Malcolm X's death flashed around the world. Thousands gathered to pay their respects outside the funeral home where his body lay. At the funeral, actor Ossie Davis said, "In honoring him, we honor the best in ourselves." One of the most powerful black men in American history had been silenced.

When *The Autobiography of Malcolm X* was published, it sold millions of copies. Today teachers still ask their students to read it and learn from it. In the 1990s, movie director Spike Lee made a movie about the life of Malcolm X, starring Denzel Washington. Today Malcolm X is recognized as one of the most important figures in recent American history.

Malcolm X was a man who went through many transformations in his life. He transformed himself from small-time criminal to spiritual leader. He also transformed himself from a man who preached hatred to one who believed that harmony between races might be possible. Malcolm X told African Americans that it was acceptable to be angry and to demand change. But in the end, his message was one of self-respect, independence, and dignity for all.

Library of Congress

TODAY MANY PEOPLE WONDER WHAT ELSE MALCOLM X COULD HAVE ACHIEVED HAD HE LIVED LONGER. NO ONE KNOWS FOR SURE, BUT WE CONTINUE TO REMEMBER AND HONOR HIM.

Timeline

1925   Malcolm Little, later known as Malcolm X, is born in Omaha, Nebraska on May 19. His parents are Earl and Louise Little.

1928   The Little family moves to Lansing, Michigan.

1929   The Littles' home is set on fire and burns to the ground as police and firefighters watch. No one is arrested for the crime. Earl Little builds a new home outside of East Lansing later that year.

1931   Malcolm starts kindergarten at Pleasant Grove Elementary School. In September, Earl Little is run over by a streetcar and dies. Rumors spread that he was murdered by white men.

1939   Louise Little has a breakdown. She will spend the next 26 years in a mental hospital. Her children are sent to live in foster homes.

1941   Malcolm moves to Boston, where he lives with his half-sister Ella. For the next few years, he will hold various jobs and move back and forth between Boston and New York City.

1946   Malcolm is arrested for theft. He is convicted and sent to Charlestown State Prison in Boston.

1947   Malcolm meets another prisoner named Bimbi, who inspires him to educate himself. Malcolm begins his own reading program in the prison library.

1948   Malcolm first learns of the Nation of Islam and the teachings of Elijah Muhammad. He is transferred to Norfolk Prison Colony, which has an excellent library.

1952   Malcolm X is released from prison. He moves to Detroit and begins attending meetings of the Nation of Islam. Elijah Muhammad encourages Malcolm to become a leader in the organization.

1953   Malcolm X becomes a minister of the Nation of Islam. He begins speaking at temples around the country.

1958   Malcolm X and Betty Sanders marry and move to Queens, New York.

1959   Newspaper and television news stories about Malcolm X begin to appear. Americans learn about the Nation of Islam and Malcolm X's message of a violent fight against racism.

1963   Elijah Muhammad tells Black Muslims not to comment on President John Kennedy's assassination. Malcolm X disobeys and speaks to reporters about the event. Muhammad restricts Malcolm X from speaking publicly, worsening disagreements between the two leaders.

1964   On March 8, Malcolm X announces that he is leaving the Nation of Islam to start his own organizations, the Muslim Mosque and the Organization of Afro-American Unity.

In April, Malcolm X leaves on a pilgrimage to Mecca. During his journey, many of his attitudes about racism and the Civil Rights Movement change. Upon his return to the United States, he begins to receive threats from Nation of Islam members who feel he has betrayed the organization.

1965   On February 14, Malcolm X's home is bombed early in the morning. On February 21, while speaking at a meeting in New York City, Malcolm X is shot 16 times. Three members of the Nation of Islam are arrested and later convicted of the crime.

The Autobiography of Malcolm X is published.

Glossary

assassinated (uh-SASS-ih-nay-ted)
When an important or famous person has been murdered, he or she has been assassinated. Malcolm X was assassinated in 1965.

boycott (BOY-kot)
A boycott is a protest in which people stop using a certain product or service. A boycott helped end segregation on public buses in Montgomery, Alabama.

breakdown (BRAYK-down)
A breakdown is a physical or mental collapse that makes it difficult for a person to function normally. After her husband's death, Louise Little suffered a breakdown.

civil rights (SIV-el RITES)
Civil rights are a person's rights to freedom and fair treatment. Malcolm X inspired people to join the struggle for civil rights.

**Civil Rights Movement
(SIV-il RITES MOOV-ment)**
The Civil Rights Movement was the struggle for equal rights for African Americans in the United States during the 1950s and 1960s. Martin Luther King Jr. was a leader in the Civil Rights Movement.

discrimination (dis-krim-ih-NAY-shun)
Discrimination is the unfair treatment of people simply because they are different. Near the end of his life, Malcolm X encouraged African Americans to work with people of other races to end discrimination.

economic (ek-uh-NOM-ik)
Economic means having to do with money or finance matters. Malcolm X believed that African Americans should achieve economic independence by supporting black people and businesses in their communities.

injustice (in-JUSS-tiss)
Injustice is something that is unfair or wrong. When people are denied equal rights, they are victims of injustice.

integrate (IN-teh-grayt)
To integrate means to bring together people who have been kept apart, especially because of race. For many years, Malcolm X did not believe that races should be integrated.

Islam (iz-LAHM)
Islam is a religion based on the teachings of the prophet Muhammad. The Nation of Islam is a U.S. religious group that bases its teachings on Islam.

militant (MIL-ih-tent)
People who are militant are fierce in their beliefs and actions. Many people considered Malcolm X militant because he thought violence might be necessary to end racism.

mosques (MOSKS)
Mosques are Muslim places of worship. The Nation of Islam built temples and mosques all over the United States.

Glossary

nonviolence (non-VY-uh-lenss)
Nonviolence is the belief that people can bring about change without hurting others. Civil rights protesters who believed in nonviolence did not respond with anger when anger was shown toward them.

oppressed (uh-PREST)
If people are oppressed, they are treated unjustly or as inferiors by others. Elijah Muhammad argued that white people wanted African Americans to remain oppressed.

pilgrimage (PIL-grim-ej)
A pilgrimage is a religious person's journey to a sacred place. Malcolm X went on a pilgrimage to the holy city of Mecca.

prophet (PROF-it)
A prophet is a religious leader who speaks as the voice of a god. Muhammad is a prophet in the religion of Islam.

racism (RAY-sih-zim)
Racism is a negative feeling or opinion about people because of their race. Malcolm X believed violence might be necessary to fight racism.

radical (RAD-ih-kul)
People who are radical want to bring about extreme change, using whatever means necessary. Elijah Muhammad thought Malcolm X was too radical.

recruit (ree-KREWT)
To recruit is to encourage someone to join an organization. Malcolm X recruited other African Americans into the Nation of Islam.

segregated (SEG-reh-gay-ted)
If people or things are segregated, they are kept apart. Many places in the United States were once segregated, so that African Americans either could not enter areas or were kept separate from white people.

Supreme Court (suh-PREEM KORT)
The Supreme Court is the highest court in the United States. In 1954, the Supreme Court ruled that schools could no longer be segregated.

transformation (trans-for-MAY-shun)
A transformation is a dramatic change. Malcolm X experienced many transformations during his lifetime.

welfare (WELL-fair)
Welfare is aid provided to needy people by the government. Louise Little accepted welfare after her husband died.

Index

Further Information

Books and Magazines

Archer, Jules. *They Had a Dream: The Civil Rights Struggle from Frederick Douglass to Marcus Garvey to Martin Luther King and Malcolm X.* New York: Puffin, 1996.

Breitman, George. *Malcolm X Speaks: Selected Speeches and Statements.* New York: Grove Press, 1999.

Davies, Mark. *Malcolm X: Another Side of the Movement* (The History of the Civil Rights Movement). New York: Silver Burdett Press, 1990.

Jeffrey, Laura S. *Betty Shabazz: Sharing the Vision of Malcolm X* (African-American Biographies). Springfield, NJ: Enslow Publishers, 2000.

Myers, Walter Dean. *Malcolm X: A Fire Burning Brightly.* New York: HarperCollins, 2000.

Shirley, David. *Malcolm X.* Broomall, PA: Chelsea House, 1994.

Venable, Rose. *The Civil Rights Movement.* Chanhassen, MN: The Child's World, 2002.

Web Sites

Find links to sites about Malcolm X:
http://www.malcolm-x.org/links.htm

Visit a site about Malcolm X from Clayton College and State University:
http://a-s.clayton.edu/Humanities/projects/literature/malcolmx/default.html

Visit the official Malcolm X Web site:
http://www.cmgww.com/historic/malcolm/bio.html

Visit a site with quotes and audio clips of Malcolm X's speeches:
http://members.aol.com/klove01/malcomsp.htm

Listen to historic speeches from Malcolm X and other civil rights leaders:
http://webcorp.com/civilrights/malcomx.htm

Visit a site about Malcolm X prepared by high school students:
http://www.geocities.com/Athens/Olympus/3515/malcx.html